This book

belongs to

German - Italian

lachen

ridere

zunge

lingua

schwenken

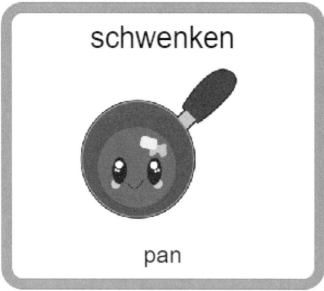

pan

fitness

fitness

löwe

leone

tag

giorno

fuchs

volpe

strauß

mazzo

wagen

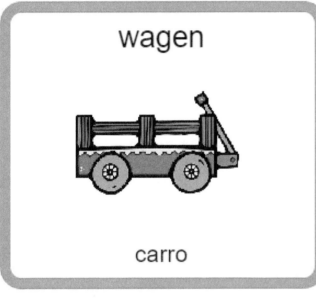

carro

fett

grasso

spritze

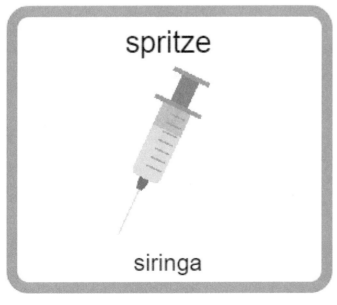

siringa

radio

radio

muschel

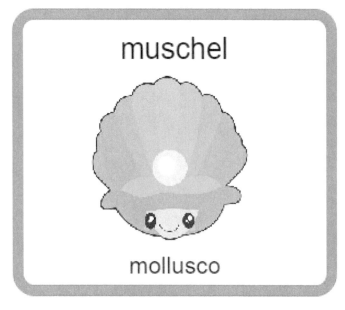

mollusco

schlafzimmer

camera da letto

boden

terra

politiker

politico

kamin

camino

uhr

orologio

traube

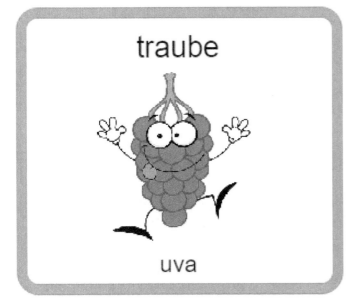

uva

maske

maschera

computers

computer

rock

gonna

matten

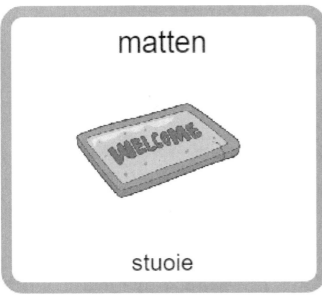

stuoie

besen

scopa

schuhe

scarpe

kirsche

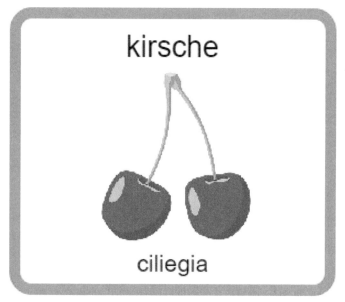

ciliegia

cowboy

cowboy

turban

turbante

fallschirm

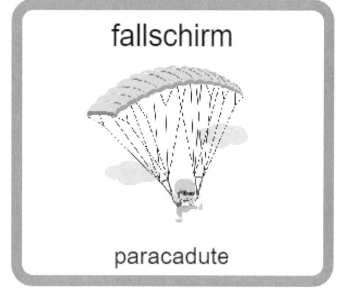

paracadute

elefant

elefante

alphabete

alfabeti

kamel

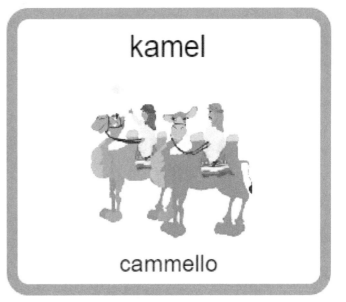

cammello

kranz

corona

hals

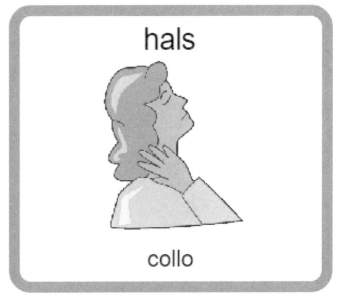

collo

zwei

due

bauernhof

fattoria

süßigkeiten

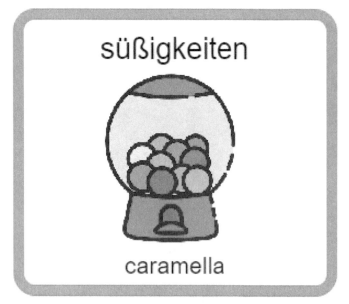

caramella

mond

luna

himbeere

lampone

milch

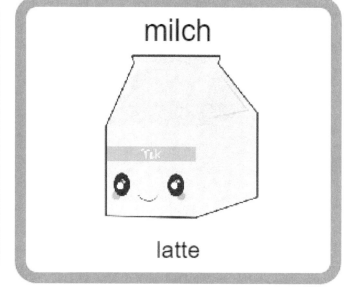

latte

tomate

pomodoro

spinne

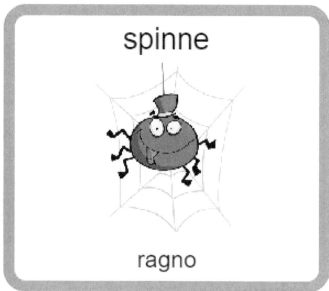

ragno

krug

brocca

wurm

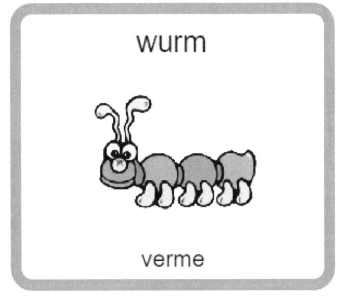

verme

weizen

grano

truthahn

tacchino

ihm

lui

aufwachen

svegliati

schüssel

ciotola

hai

squalo

smoking

smoking

zebra

zebra

stinktiere

puzzole

wütend

arrabbiato

verbergen

nascondere

vater

padre

karren

carriola

kiwi

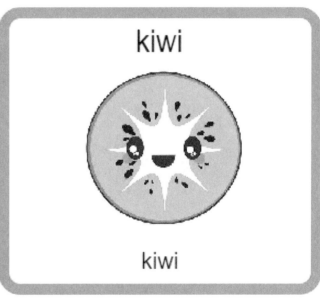

kiwi

spielzeug

giocattolo

traurig

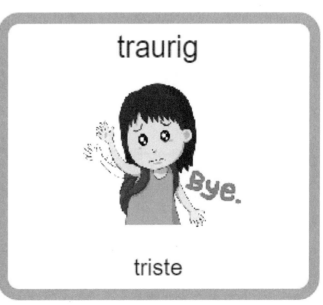

triste

schloss

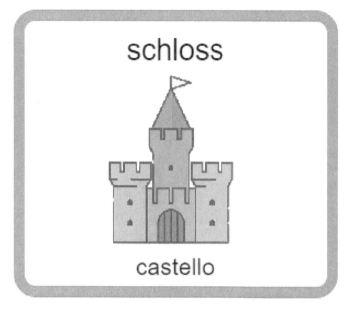

castello

kreis

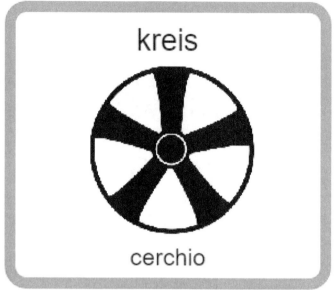

cerchio

krank

malato

leguan

iguana

zupfen

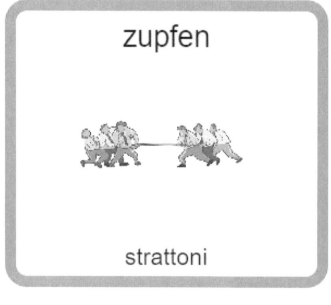

strattoni

laterne

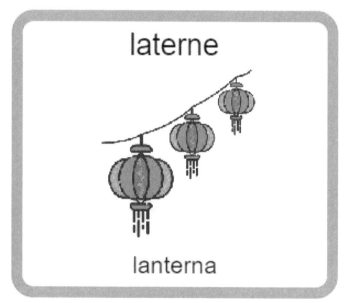

lanterna

leiter

scala

kröte

rospo

mädchen

ragazza

schaufeln

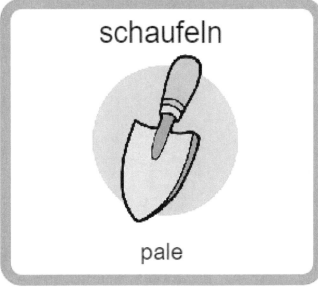

pale

frisch

fresco

klingen

suono

klettern

arrampicata

monster

mostro

bart

barba

maulwurf

talpa

dressing

condimento

spiegel

specchio

perücke

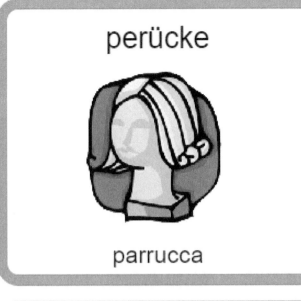

parrucca

auge

occhio

stand

stare in piedi

regenbogen

arcobaleno

essen

mangiare

portion

servendo

ein

uno

geier

avvoltoio

zahn

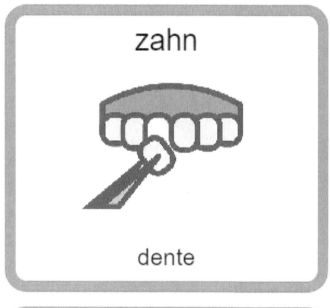

dente

lehrer

insegnante

umarmung

abbraccio

fenster

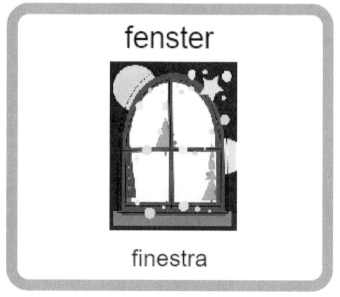

finestra

pelikan

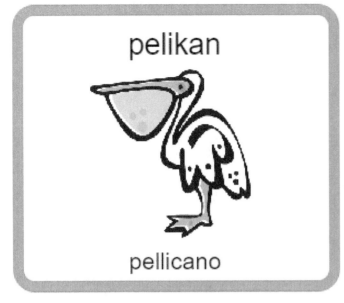

pellicano

rechen

rastrello

alligator

alligatore

boxen

boxe

die glühbirne

lampadina

sitzen

sedersi

affe

scimmia

eis am stiel

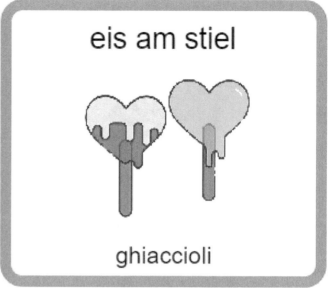

ghiaccioli

gesichter

facce

granatapfel

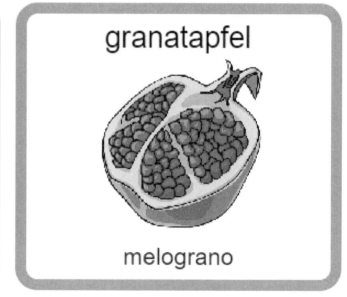

melograno

hexen

streghe

hüfte

anca

kompass

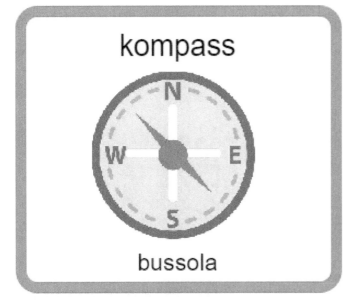

bussola

singen

cantando

donuts

ciambelle

stift

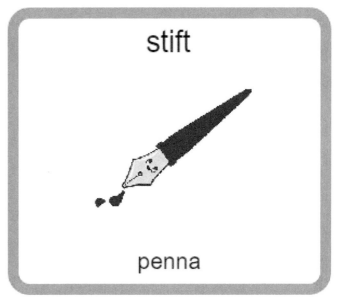

penna

müll

spazzatura

lippenstift

rossetto

schmutz

sporco

museum

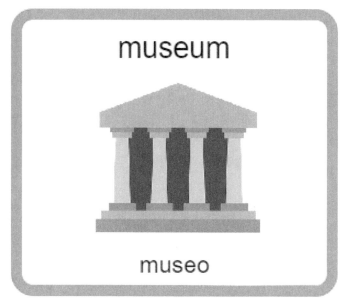

museo

salat

insalata

wissenschaft

scienza

karosserie

corpo

stute

cavalla

unheimlich

pauroso

honig

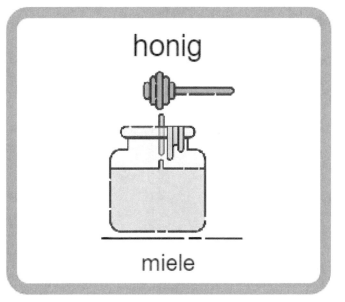

miele

pferd

cavallo

fotograf

fotografo

vase

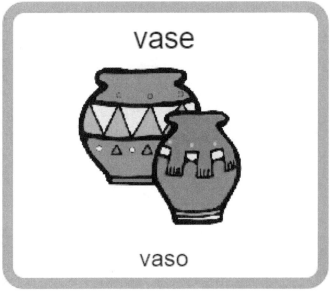

vaso

iglu

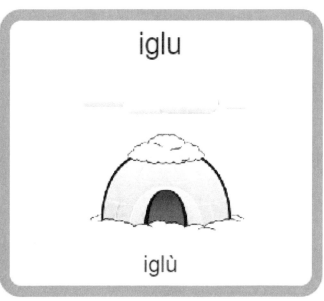

iglù

hügel

collina

kaffee

caffè

mops

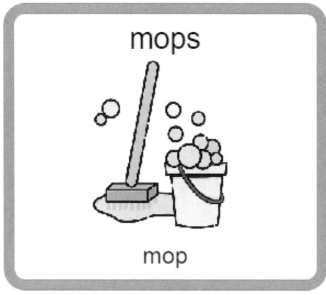

mop

auberginen

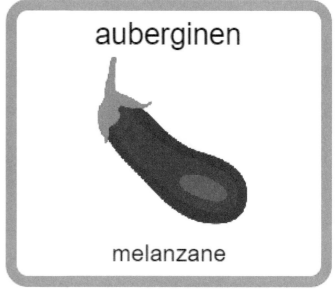

melanzane

igel

riccio

holz

legna

süß

carina

gorilla

gorilla

baum

albero

strümpfe

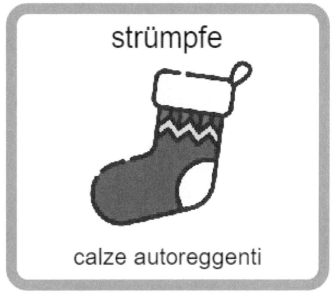

calze autoreggenti

lauf

correre

familie

famiglia

ball

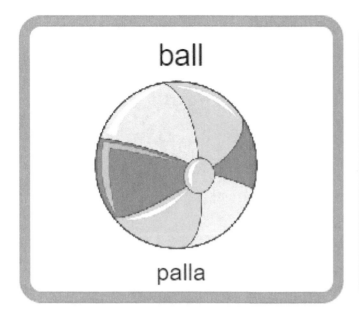

palla

künstler

artista

schal

sciarpa

kätzchen

gattino

springen

saltare

schule

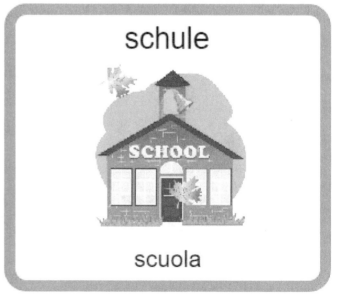

scuola

hase

coniglio

schläger

racchetta

tiere

animali

schwester

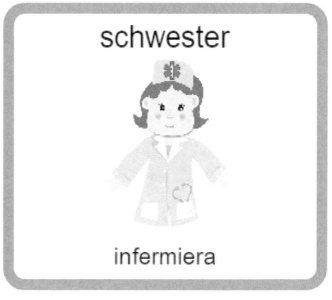

infermiera

toilette

gabinetto

riechen

odore

eishockey

hockey

pirat

pirata

erbsen

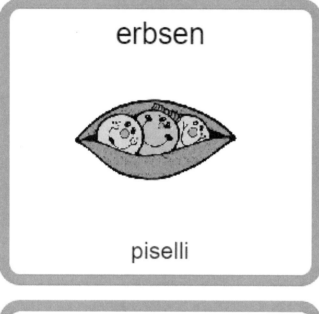

piselli

bus

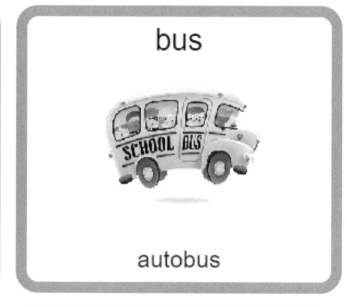

autobus

buntstifte

pastelli

küche

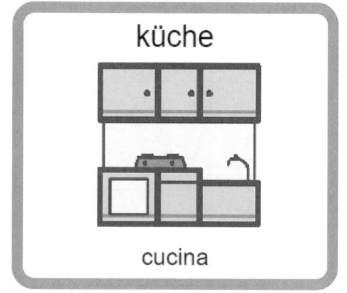

cucina

würfel

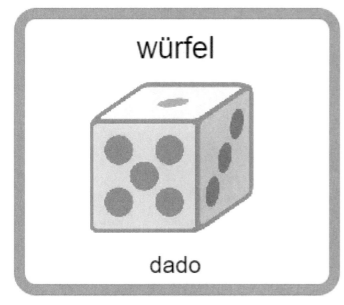

dado

diamant

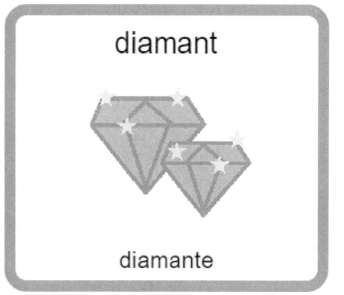

diamante

schreiben

scrittura

sieg

vincere

fabrik

fabbrica

daumen

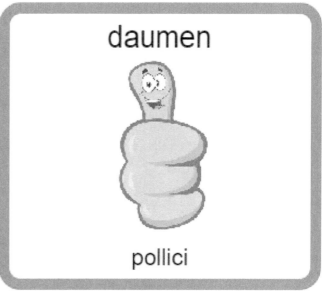

pollici

krabbe

granchio

fehler

insetto

sieben

sette

kuh

mucca

respekt

rispetto

schlagen

colpire

mais

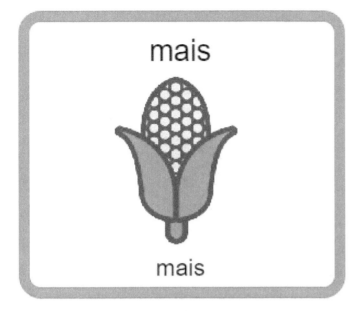

mais

quiz

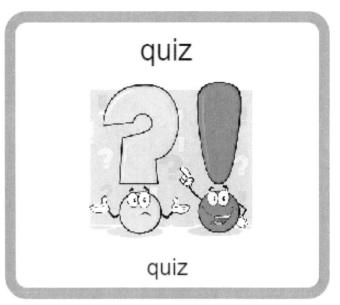

quiz

deckel

coperchi

behälter

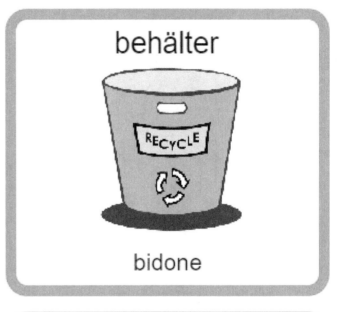

bidone

hirsch

cervo

blume

fiore

apfel

mela

sofa

divano

gehirne

mente

mutter

madre

utensilien

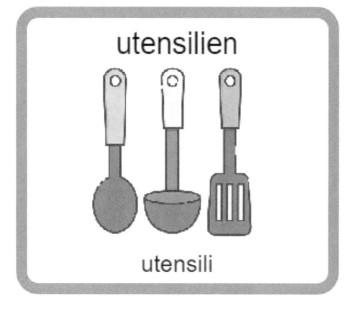

utensili

känguru

canguro

gewehr

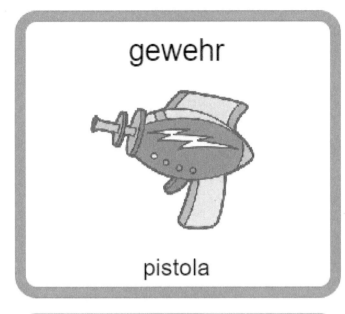

pistola

preise

premi

grapefruit

pompelmo

erdnuss

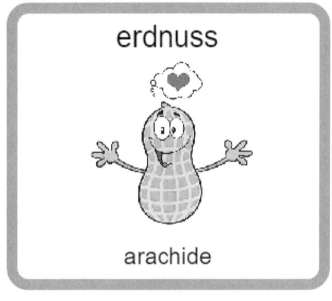

arachide

spatel

spatola

kinder

bambini

stricken

maglieria

rübe

rapa

schildkröte

tartaruga

eber

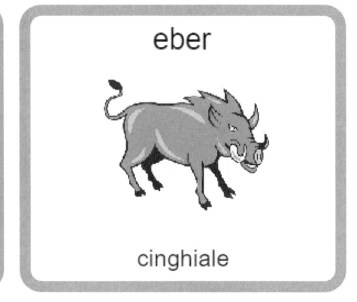

cinghiale

boot

barca

kuchen

torta

mächtig

potente

schere

forbici

vulkan

vulcano

mann

uomo

fackel
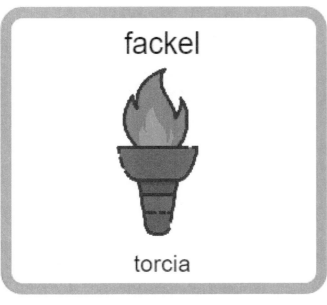
torcia

katze

gatto

donner

tuono

socken

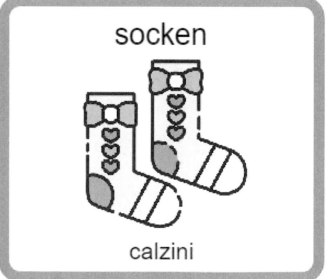

calzini

staub

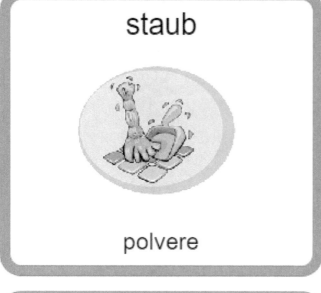

polvere

verbieten

vietare

geister

fantasmi

schneeflocke

fiocco di neve

nase

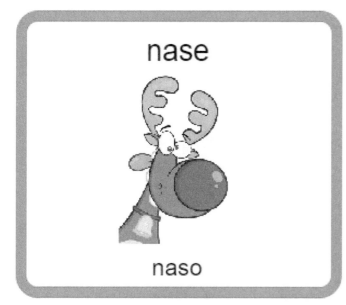

naso

basketball

pallacanestro

mathematik

matematica

handtuch

salvietta

cafe

caffè

flosse

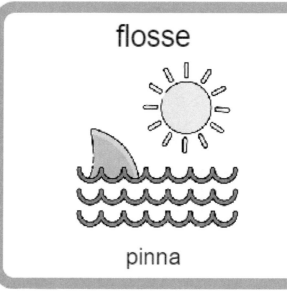

pinna

bäcker

panettiere

hut

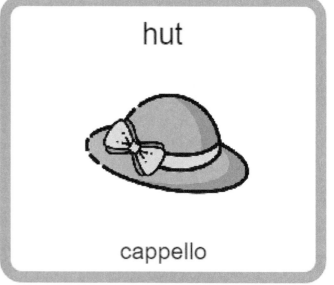

cappello

geschenk

regali

whiskey

whisky

reifen

pneumatico

bär

orso

halt

fermare

karten

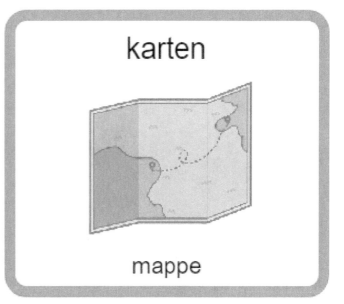

mappe

marmelade

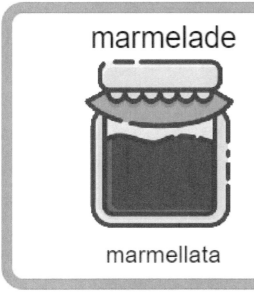

marmellata

oval

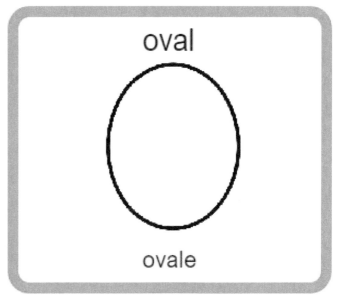

ovale

klatschen

applaudire

golf

golf

eicheln

ghiande

bitten

elemosinare

polizist

poliziotto

zeichnung

disegno

murmeltier

marmotta

lotus

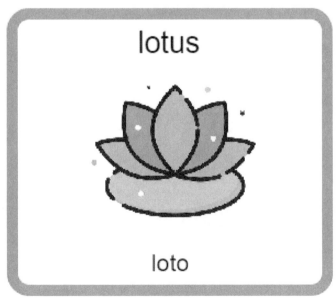

loto

wurst

salsiccia

ziehen

traino

schnee

la neve

junge

ragazzo

insel

isola

brokkoli

broccoli

rennen

gara

ebene

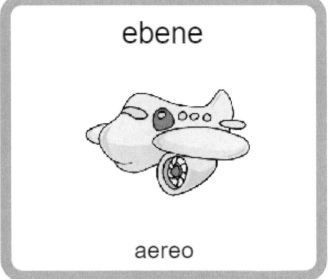

aereo

drei

tre

eier

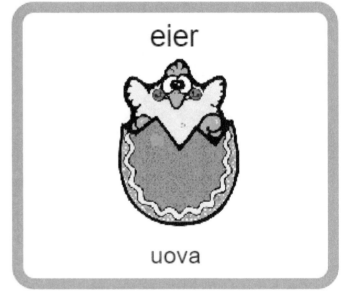

uova

couch

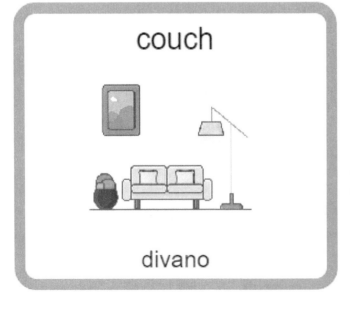

divano

treffen

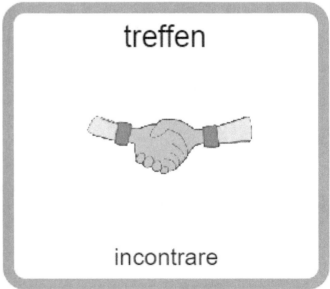

incontrare

rakete

razzo

kaktus
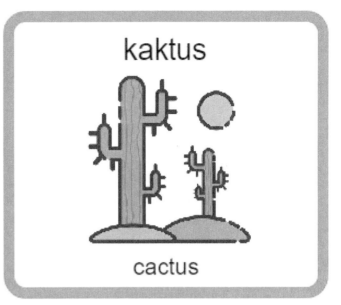
cactus

knabbern

sgranocchiare

schlange

serpente

nachrichten

notizia

saft

succo

pflanzen

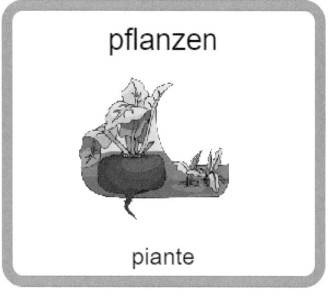

piante

fleisch

carne

beeindrucken

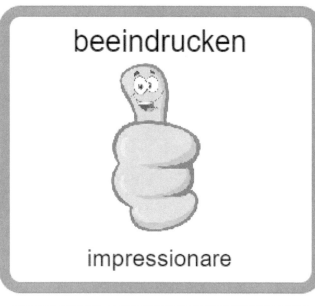

impressionare

suchen

sguardo

fußball

calcio

felsen

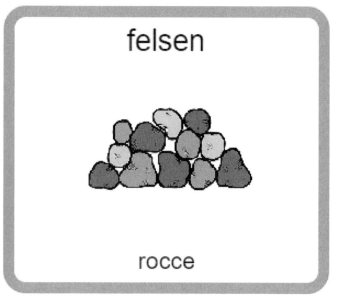

rocce

beine

gambe

kragen

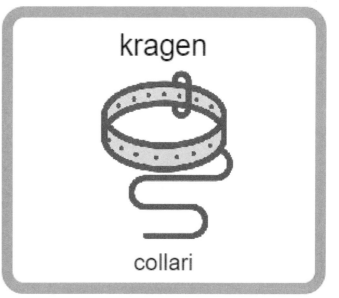

collari

übel

mali

drachen

aquilone

ballon

ballon

klavier

pianoforte

polizist

poliziotto

gurke

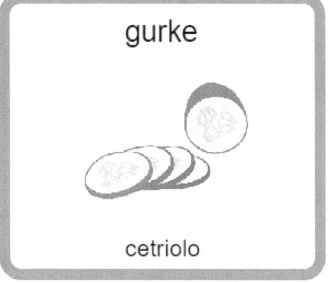

cetriolo

mandarine

mandarino

nixe

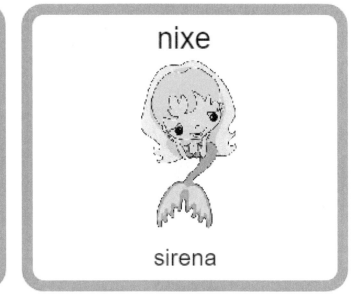

sirena

vorhänge

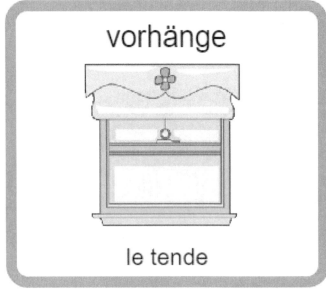

le tende

mund

bocca

fernrohr
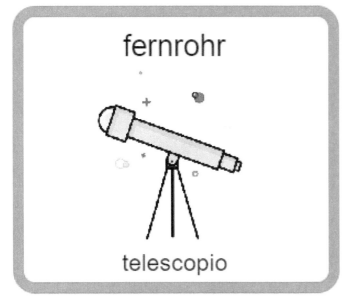
telescopio

jeeps

jeep

heringe
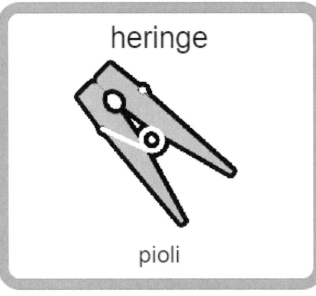
pioli

regen

pioggia

paare

coppie

shorts
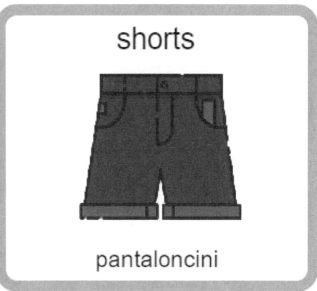
pantaloncini

gelangweilt

annoiato

wachtel

quaglia

sechs

sei

party

festa

arzt

medico

sandwiches

panini

schaf

pecora

gitarre

chitarra

lieferung

consegna

stiefel

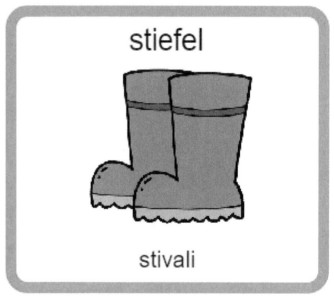

stivali

metzger

macellaio

schnecke

lumaca

papier

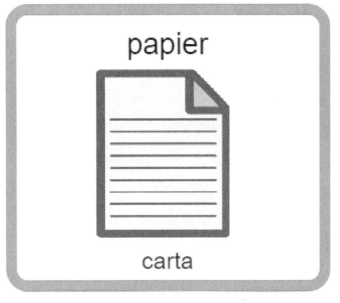

carta

nudeln

tagliatelle

stolz

orgoglioso

heiß

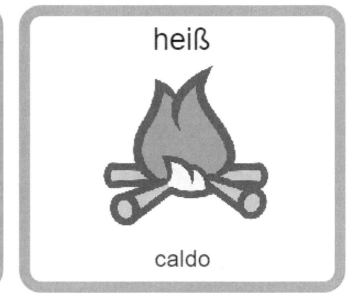

caldo

van

furgone

roller

scooter

stuhl

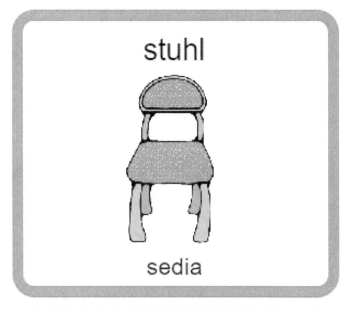

sedia

schinken

prosciutto

strauß

struzzo

mäuse

topi

brieftasche

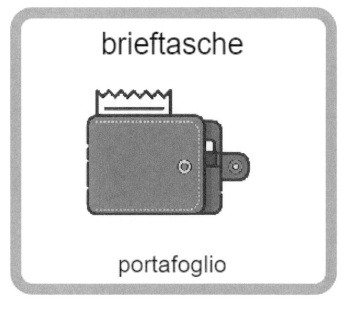

portafoglio

lied

canzone

hammer

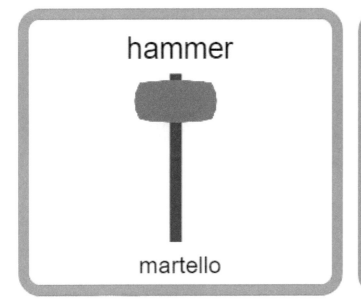

martello

kleben

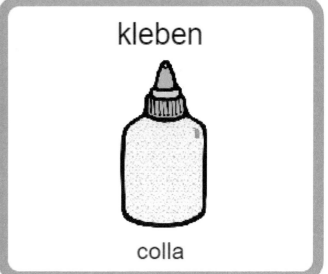

colla

könig

re

schulter

spalla

delphin

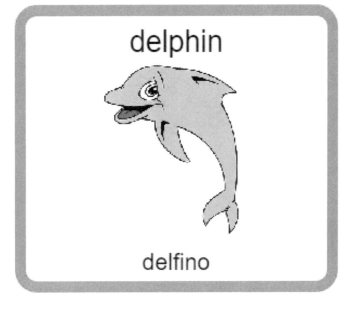

delfino

unter

sotto

verletzt

male

adler

aquila

muskel

muscolo

schlafen

sonno

genießen

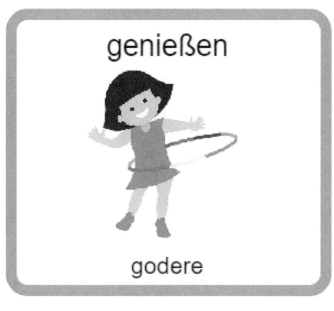

godere

rot

rosso

unzufrieden

infelice

bomben

bombe

angeln

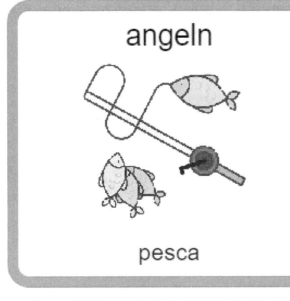

pesca

tasche

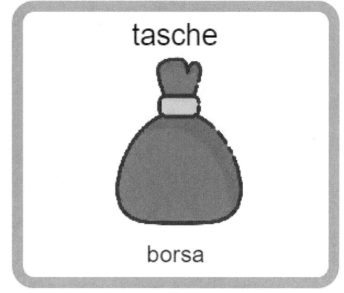

borsa

abwischen

asciugandosi

teppiche

tappeti

pudding

budino

strand

spiaggia

perlen

perle

farbe

dipingere

pfeile
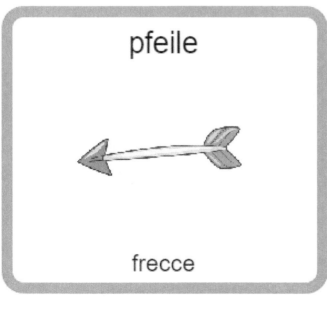
frecce

freundlich

amichevole

küken

pulcini

null
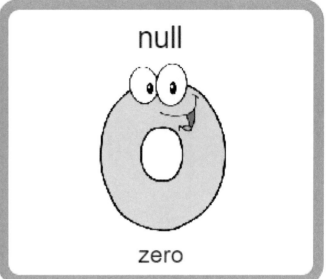
zero

klinik
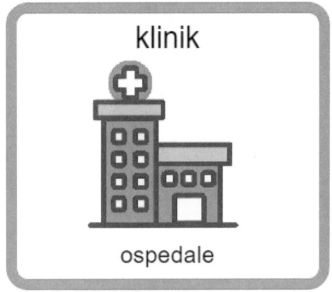
ospedale

klebt

bastoni

limonade

soda

koala
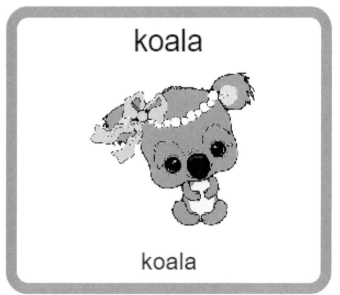
koala

taxi

taxi

ofen

forno

erde

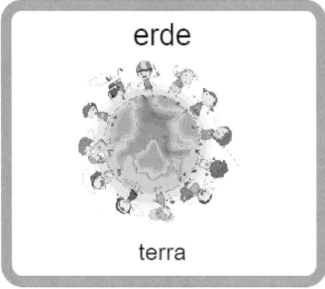

terra

lampen

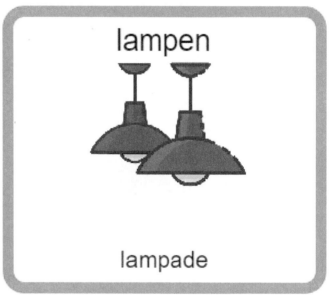

lampade

wedeln

burlone

insekt

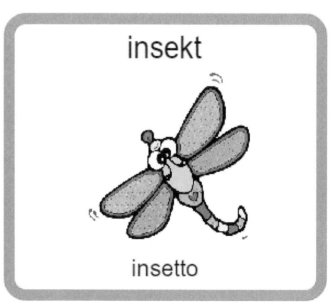

insetto

rose

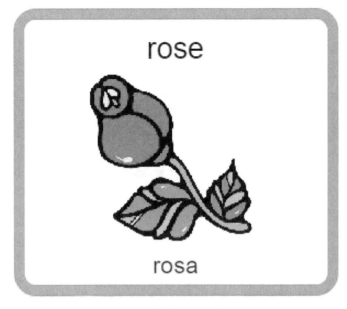

rosa

puppe

bambola

reiten

equitazione

badewanne

vasca da bagno

taschentuch

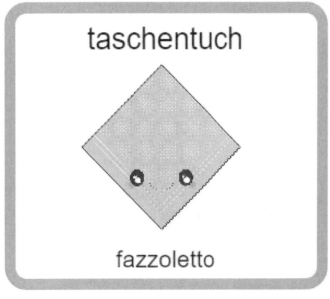

fazzoletto

birnen

pere

bild

immagine

tablett

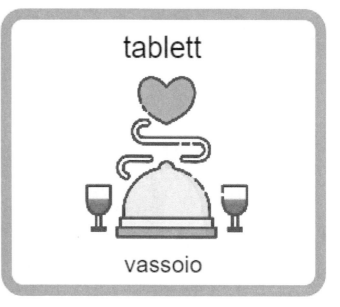

vassoio

steppdecken

trapunte

straße

strada

knochen

osso

scheu

timida

tafel

lavagna

duschen

la doccia

gehen

camminare

suppe

la minestra

eis

ghiaccio

zwiebel

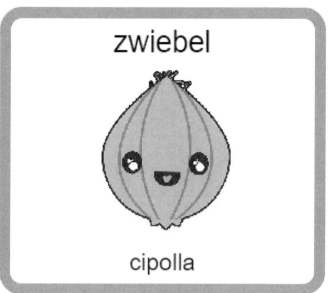

cipolla

lehren

insegnare

zitrone

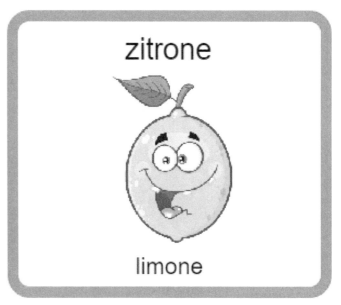

limone

auf wiedersehen

addio

pullover

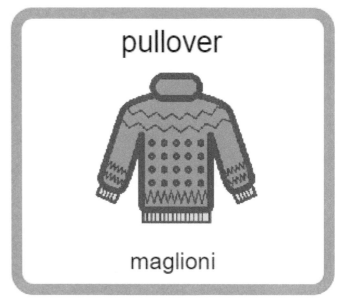

maglioni

frosch

rana

rucksack

zaino

erdbeere

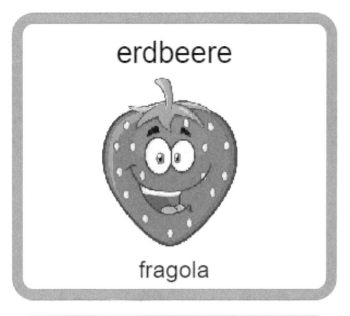

fragola

ziege

capra

nest

nido

banane

banana

hüpfen

saltellando

giraffe

giraffa

tinten

inchiostri

ananas

ananas

kamera

telecamera

handschuhe

guanti

kartoffel

patata

brille

bicchieri

kniend

in ginocchio

hochzeit

nozze

regenschirm

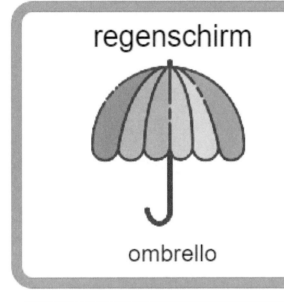

ombrello

ente

anatra

pumps

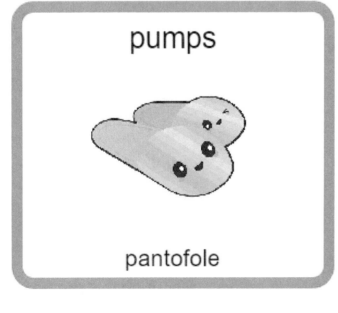

pantofole

musik

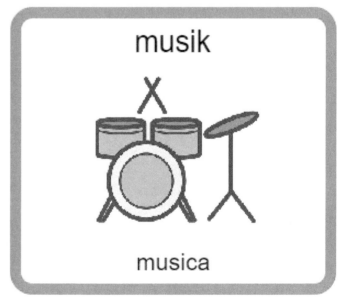

musica

baby

bambino

eis

gelato

fass

barile

lächeln

sorriso

feiern

celebrare

herd

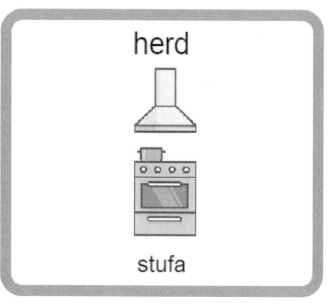

stufa

bleistift

matita

medizin

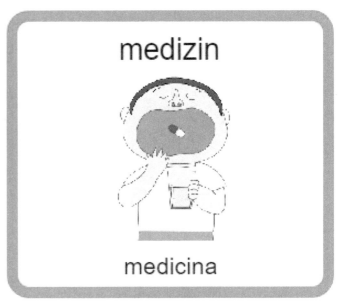

medicina

ziemlich

bella

fütterung

alimentazione

käfig

gabbia

star

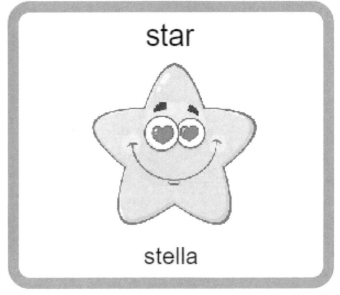

stella

chili

chili

weihnachten

natale

abspielen

giocare

geschenke

i regali

morgen

mattina

engel

angelo

rauben

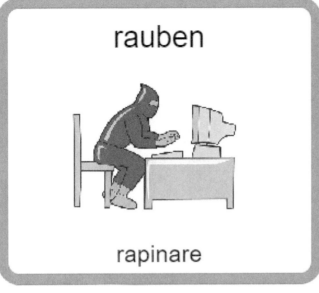

rapinare

tintenfisch

polpo

paket

pacchetto

junges

cucciolo

kinderbett

culla

gepard

ghepardo

spiele

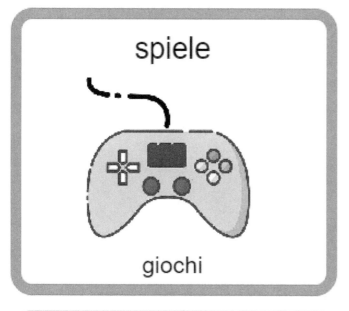

giochi

orange

arancia

schreibtisch

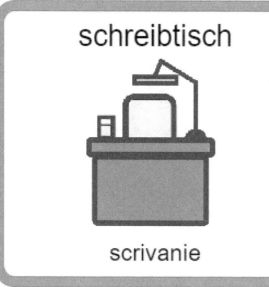

scrivanie

boden

suolo

zaun

recinto

aggressiv

aggressivo

schwanz

coda

bett

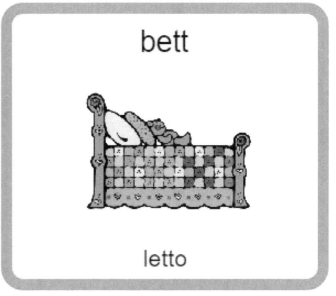

letto

hexagon

Hexagon

esagono

neun

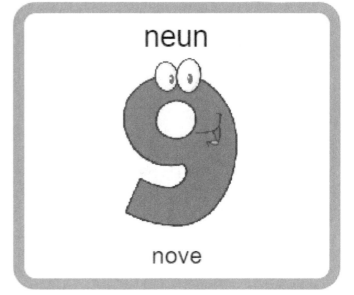

nove

verringern

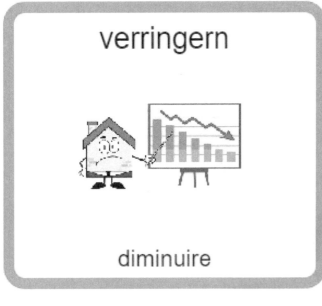

diminuire

tassen

tazze

ellbogen

gomito

papagei

pappagallo

palme

palma

panda

panda

waschen

lavaggio

schwein

maiale

ritter

cavaliere

glocke

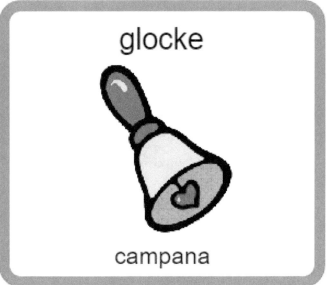

campana

hemd

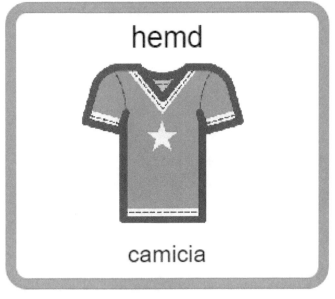

camicia

sommer

estate

punkte

punti

avocado

avocado

stinkend

puzzolente

topf

pentola

kochen

cucinando

messer

coltello

baseball

baseball

podium

podio

stachelschwein

porcospino

werfen

lancio

korb

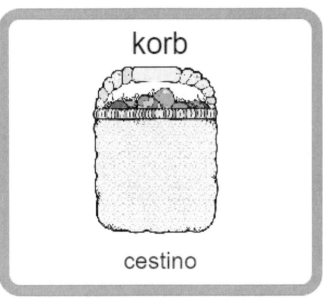

cestino

flugzeug

aereo

pinsel

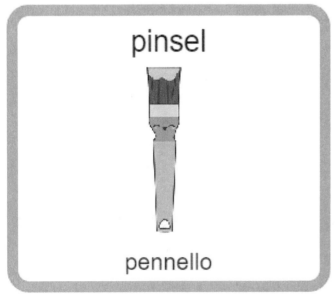

pennello

tiger

tigre

teppich

tappeto

sauber

pulito

hotel

hotel

kalender

calendario

hahn

gallo

stilvoll

elegante

brief
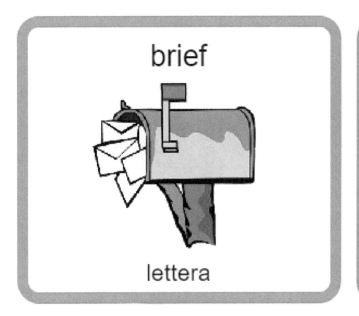
lettera

wassermelone
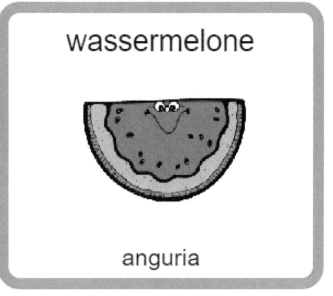
anguria

grabstein

lapide

tanzen

danza

fallen

autunno

koch

capocuoco

lineal

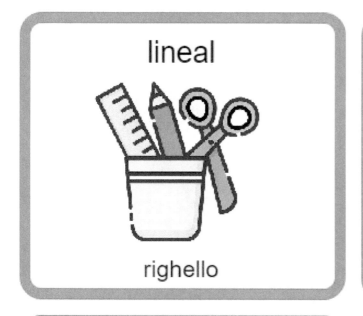

righello

geige

violino

aktentasche

ventiquattrore

eimer

secchio

kopf

capo

cutter

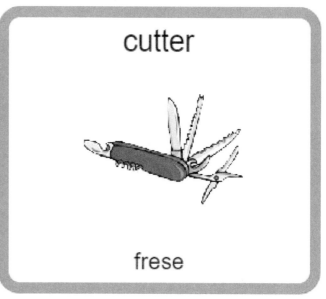

frese

tasse

tazza

weinen

piangere

schmetterling

farfalla

kirche

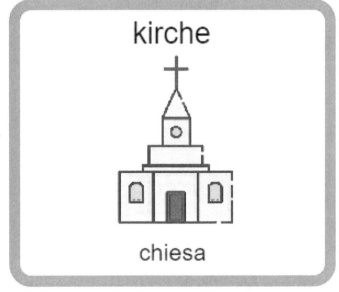

chiesa

haar

capelli

vier

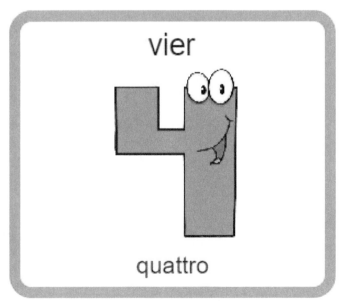

quattro

auto

auto

kokosnuss

cocco

geld

i soldi

mannschaft

squadra

papa

papà

brot

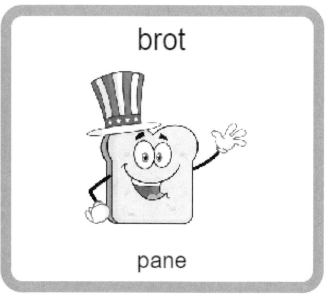

pane

impfstoff

vaccino

zahlen

numeri

hand

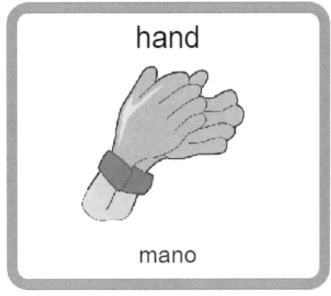

mano

ruhig

silenzioso

windmühle

mulini a vento

unterstände

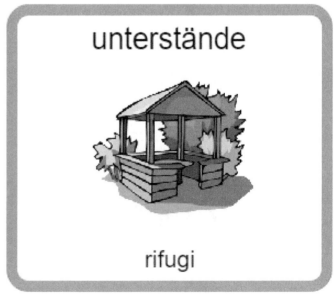

rifugi

ameise

formica

abendessen

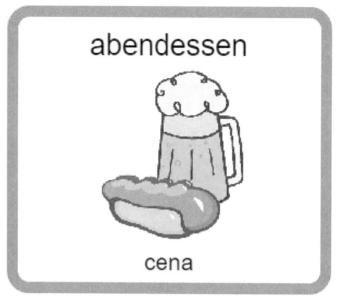

cena

freund

amico

wal

balena

führer

capi

einhorn

unicorno

beißen

mordere

saat

semi

tee

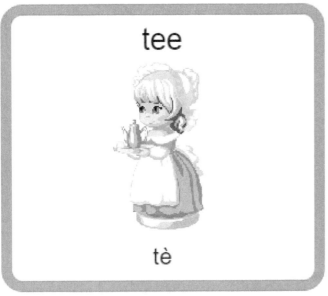

tè

taschenrechner

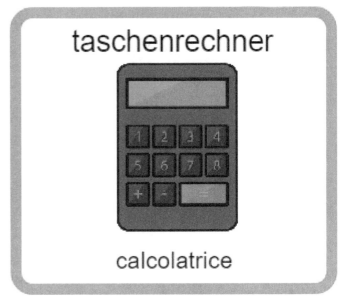

calcolatrice

zauberer

mago

anker

ancora

bücherregal

scaffale

mixer

miscelatore

teekanne

teiera

stark

forte

hanteln

manubri

motor

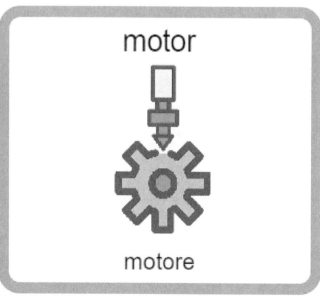

motore

kinder

bambini

hündchen

cucciolo

reißverschluss

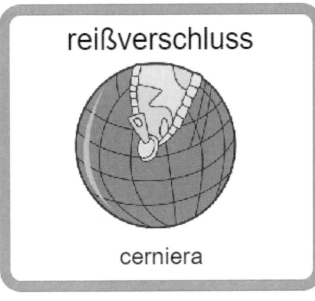

cerniera

bohne

fagiolo

kerzen

candele

finger

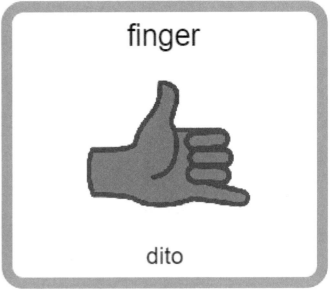

dito

arbeiten

lavoro

wasser
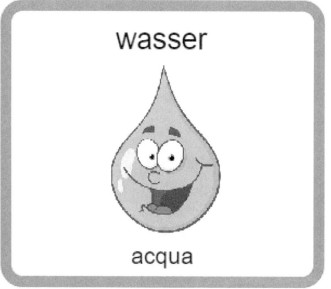
acqua

kissen
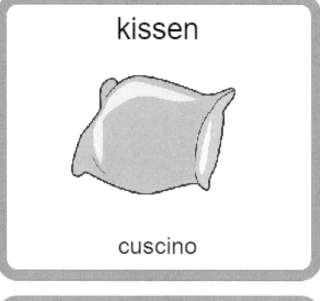
cuscino

fisch

pesce

ohrring
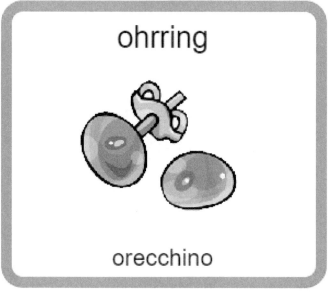
orecchino

zelte
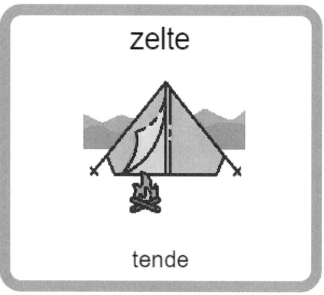
tende

eichhörnchen

scoiattoli

massagen

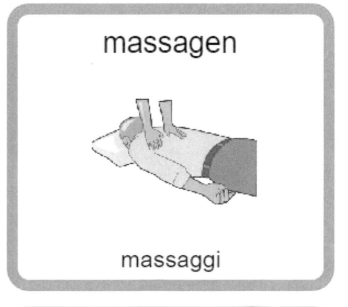

massaggi

pflaume

prugna

garten

giardino

hilfe

aiuto

maid

domestica

pyjama

pigiama

plätzchen

biscotto

gemüse

verdure

joghurt

yogurt

hallo

ciao

blatt

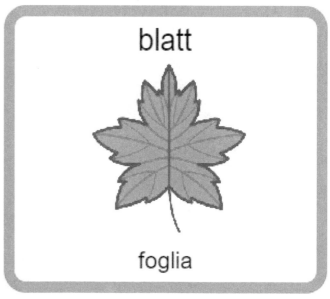

foglia

gras

erba

kellner

camerieri

biene

ape

lesen

lettura

steak

bistecca

fahrrad

bicicletta

rentier

renna

axt

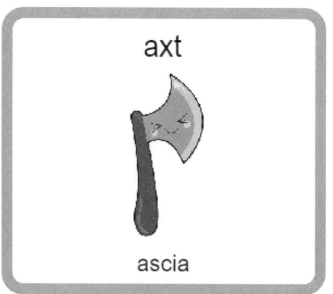

ascia

frage

domanda

untergang

naufragio

fliegt

mosche

yak

yak

schnuller

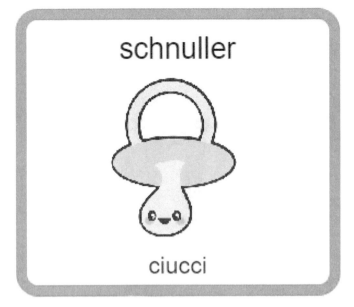

ciucci

henne

gallina

botschaft

messaggio

nickerchen

pisolino

stift

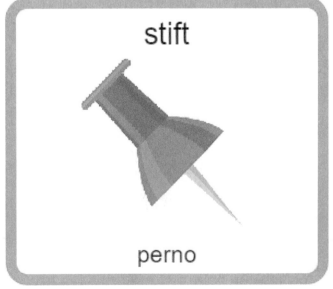

perno

pinguin

pinguino

wind

vento

segelboot

barca a vela

acht

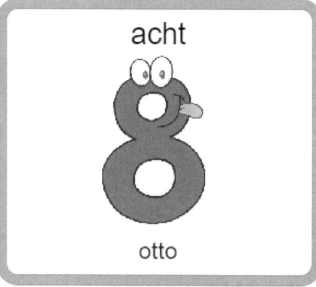

otto

zähne

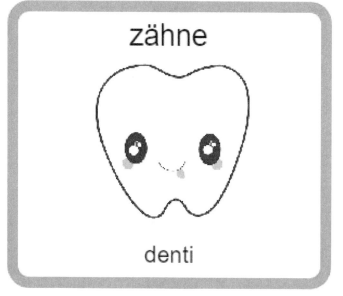

denti

zähmen

domare

mama

mamma

froh

gioioso

gürtel

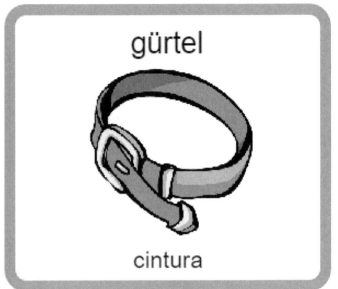

cintura

fünf

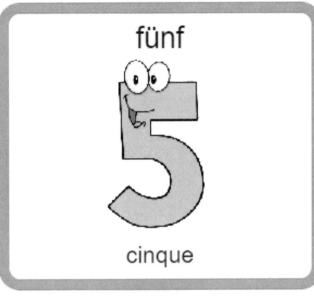

cinque

arm

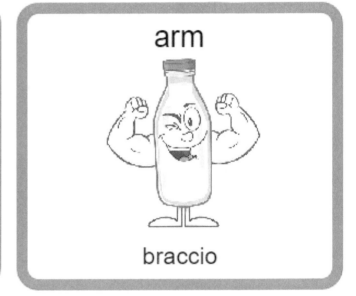

braccio

farmer

contadino

käse

formaggio

schwimmen

nuoto

hähnchen

pollo

ratte

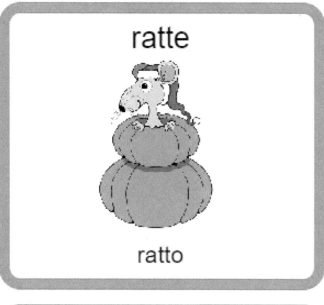

ratto

bügeln

stiro

sonne

sole

pizza

pizza

königin

regina

fahrrad

bicicletta

groß

grande

dock

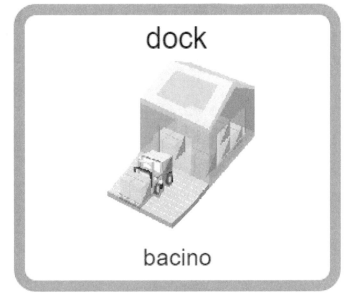

bacino

graben

scavare

eule

gufo

joggen

jogging

öffnen

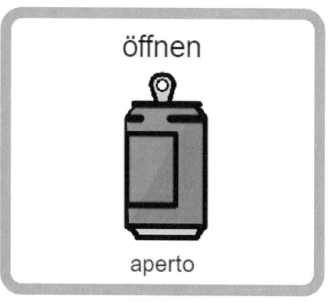

aperto

garn

filato

nilpferd

ippopotamo

herbst

autunni

medikation

medicazione

laut

forte

berge

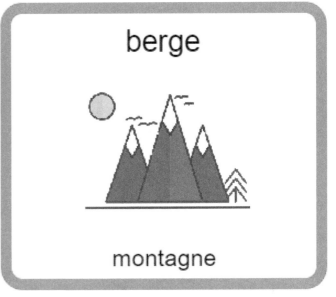

montagne

teetasse

tazza di tè

lätzchen

bavaglino

brücke

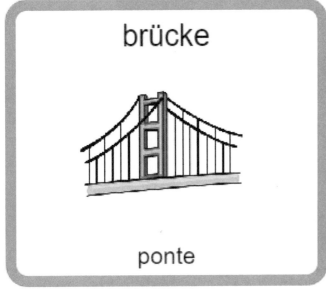

ponte

ring

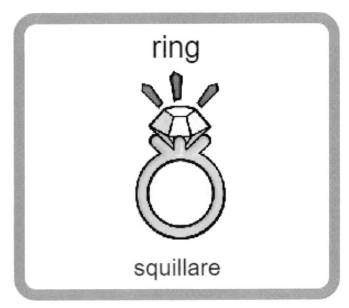

squillare

gut

bene

kleinkinder

bambini

schläfrig

assonnato

manager

manager

kamin

camino

köstlich

delizioso

backstein

mattone

halskette

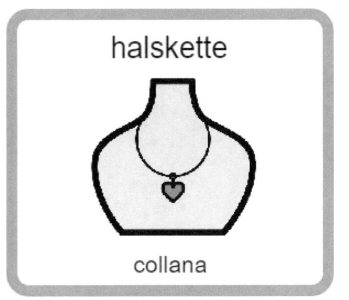

collana

buch

libro

säcke

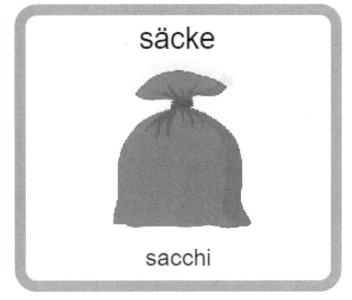

sacchi

mikroskop

microscopio

getränk

bere

blut

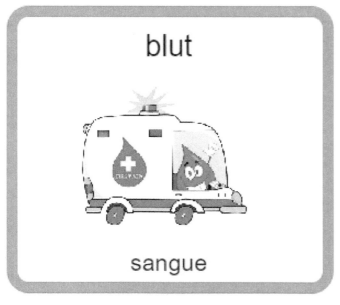

sangue

feuer

fuoco

fahren

guida

weste

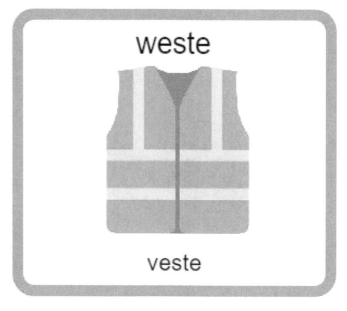

veste

musiker

musicista

nacht

notte

tür

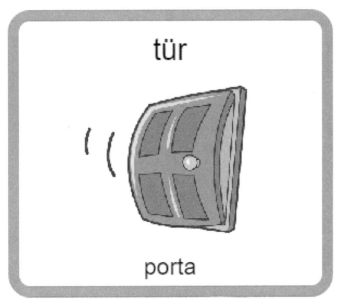

porta

mantel

cappotto

schlecht

male

ketchup

ketchup

nass

bagnato

nüsse

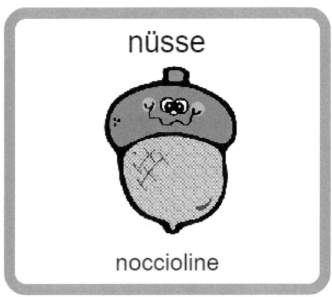

noccioline

pfirsich

pesca

prinzessin

principessa

schneiden

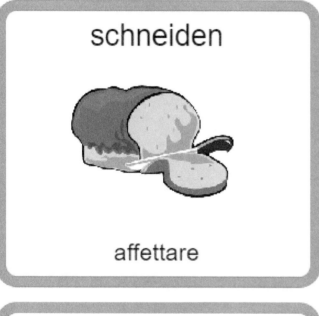

affettare

ohren

orecchie

bruder

fratello

koffer

valigia

lastwagen

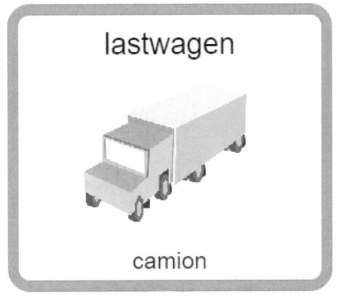

camion

glücklich

contento

pfütze

pozzanghera

liebe

amore

hund

cane

haus

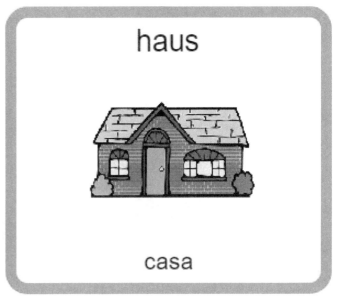

casa

flagge

bandiera

barbier

barbiere

züge

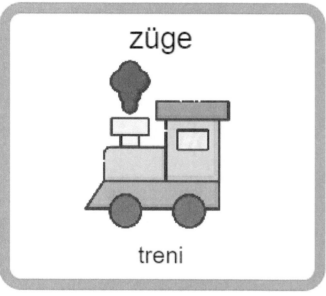

treni

pagode

pagoda

eidechse

lucertola

benzin

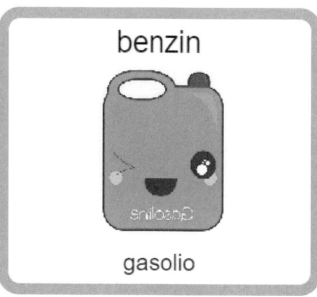

gasolio

schwester

sorella

flasche

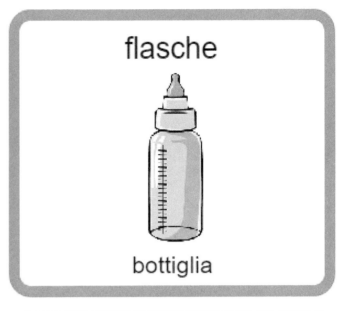

bottiglia

helm

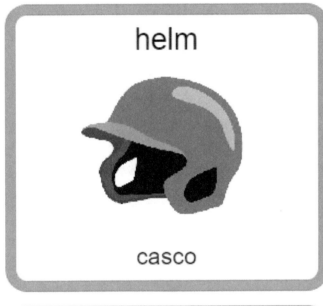

casco

jacke

giacca

skizzieren

schizzo

schokolade

cioccolato

pilz

fungo

kleider

abiti

kamm

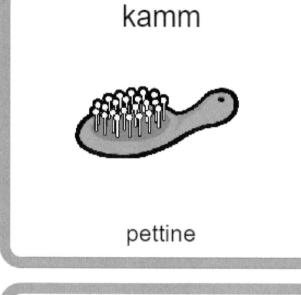

pettine

kuchen

——————— ——

torte

karotte

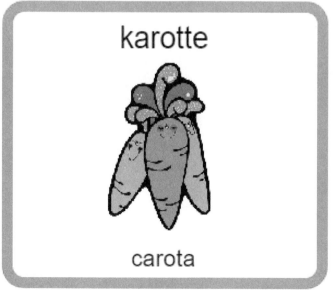

carota

walross

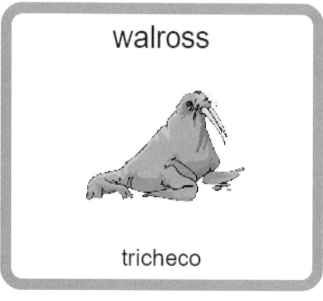

tricheco

studieren

studiando

schwan

cigno

auster

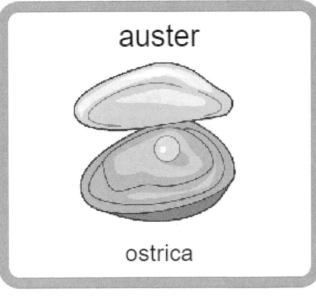

ostrica

einkaufen

shopping

zehn

dieci

taube

piccione

oben

su

mikrofon

microfono

wütend

pazzo

unterschrift

firma

box

scatola

wolf

lupo

Printed in France by Amazon
Brétigny-sur-Orge, FR